r's paraphrase.

ublication Data

ria Gaither.

hard cover)

8

Photography
na

Thinkpen Design, Inc.

015

To Julie —
Prayer is never
more beautiful than when it's
lived out over the long haul. Keep
praying! Love,

Published by
Gaither Music Group
1703 South Park Avenue
Alexandria, IN 46001
www.gaither.com
Printed in the U.S.A.

All Scripture quoted herein is the autho

Library of Congress Cataloging-in-P
Gaither, Gloria.
A book of simple prayers / Glo
p. cm.
ISBN 978-0-941565-02-8
1. Prayers. I. Titl
BV245.G348 200
242'.8—dc22
2008006858

Author photo by Nancy's
Anderson, India

Book cover design & typesetting

Reprint: June

a book

of simple

prayers

by
Gloria Gaither

Gaither Music Group
Alexandria, Indiana.

*For all the dear ones who faithfully
prayed for me and still do—
some who share my story here
and some who now see and live
the scope of the Big Story.*

Author's Note

I never intended to write this book. In fact, I never started out to write prayers. But there was a span of time when prayers came whenever I began to write. I could not begin whatever project was before me until I cleared my mind of the prayer that was tumbling from my heart onto the page. Up to that time, I had not had a similar experience, and have not since.

At first I kept them in a small pocket-sized notebook, but soon the notebook was full and the prayers kept pouring out. I treasured them and kept them hidden, reading them sometimes in my most private times. I thought my journey was unique and much too personal to reveal to anyone else.

But as the months and now years have passed, I am coming to know that my story is not unique. It is not even my own, but a story within a much larger story. It is, in fact, only the larger Story that has given meaning to my days. I am coming to believe that it is the Owner of the larger Story to whom I am drawn, the One to whom my heart instinctively cries.

I believe this One is both my origin and my destination, and the more I come to recognize my story's place in the grander Story, my once bewildered questions are turning to psalms of thanksgiving at the wonder of being so wondrously included.

As you look at these, the snapshots of my story unfolding over the course of a year or two, I hope you catch a glimpse of the Author behind it all.

1
Restore my soul, O God

Restore my soul, O God—
Breathe life back into my deflated lungs—
Pour water into my tissues, for I am depleted of Your spirit,
   I am dehydrated of the Water of Life.
I am ravenous with hunger, yet I am weak and too weary
   to search for food.

Take me by the hand and lead me to Your supply.
I am not asking for manna dropping from the sky—
I'm not asking for streams gushing from a desert rock—
I don't need a miracle to make me believe—
I know You, Yourself, are the nourishment I need.
Lead me to You, God.
Your Son has already left the pantry door open—
Give me a hand and lead me in that direction.

2
I praise You, O God

I praise You, O God,
For giving every creature what it needs.
The gulls float on the ocean that is teeming with fish.
    They walk the sandy beach where Your waves have carried
        and buried scallops and clams.
The fish swim where the minnow
        and tiny shrimp hatch in over-sufficient numbers.

The whales find what they need in each gulp of seawater . . .
　　and it's already salted!
For the plant-eaters, there is kelp.
The dove picking along the grasses finds the seeds of the grasses,
　　while the pelican scoops along with his sharp eyes
　　　　that spot a silvery movement in the water
　　　　　　a hundred feet away.
Am I, too, sitting right on top of what I need?
Has the marvel of Your provision placed me
　　in the richest feeding ground
　　　　for my particular hungers?
Forgive me for expecting more miracles when I am a miracle,
　　living in a bed of miracles.
Today You will feed me where I am.

3
Come when my lips tell You to go

Come; come when my lips tell You to go.

Come, when I turn my back and walk away.

Come, when I embrace the night;

    come bring the dawn of some new day.

Come with natal freshness when my soul is withered,
  dry with age—
When I am stuck within my story,
  come thou hand that turns the page.
Come, thou tides of restless mercy,
  wash up on my shifting sand.
Come when I, unsteady, waver—
  be the strong and staying hand.
I—unfaithful, fickle—wander after glitter, charming grace—
  come, throw pretense into shadow
by the blinding beauty of Your face.

4
Make me sensitive to the vibrations

Make me sensitive to the vibrations of the souls
    that sound around me.
The sounds a soul makes are often faint . . . and tentative.
If I am not listening, I may not hear them at all.
Let me hear the broken chords,
    the notes slightly out of tune.
Sometimes mouths make noise loud and brash
    to cover the quivering tones of the injured soul.

Let me listen for hurting whimpers
    between the blasts of bawdy jokes
        and boisterous brags.
Tune the strings of my own heart, Lord, so they may vibrate
    in sympathetic tones to the timid, tentative tunes
        of children and novices.
When soul sounds are out of range
    for my human receptive capabilities,
        may the vibrations around me,
            bypassing my instrument,
                move my spirit.
And when I hurry down life's thoroughfare
    past a pocket of joyful sounds,
        let me stop to dance!

5
You can only produce good things

Lord, You can only produce good things.

You said that when I am grafted into You, it is Your life that flows,

Your sap coming from Your vine that feeds me, the branch.

The buds, the flowers, the fruit that grows on my branch

are natural results of Your living fluids keeping me alive.

How, then, can I produce bad fruit?

How can I produce any fruit?

When I disconnect from You, I'm a dead stick.

When I remain grafted and growing, I produce Your fruit.

So if there is fruit,
    I am in You and the fruit is always good.

If there is no fruit, I am kindling. That's all.

Be my life, Lord, and I will share Your fruit with anyone
    who is hungry.

Make my fruit grow profusely because no scar tissue in the graft
    obstructs the life-flow.

6
Bless the children

Bless the children.
Bless their questions and their un-jaded answers.
Bless their hands that hold my face
 and peer guilelessly into my eyes.
Bless their lips that kiss without embarrassment,
 their arms that hug without restraint,
 their mouths that shape the deep truth in simple words—
 "I love you."

Bless their minds that know no roadblocks
  to their quest for knowledge,
    no obstacles to their curiosity,
      and no cynicism to block their trust.
While they still know purely, let the children teach us.
While they believe openly, let the children pray for us.
While they trust without restriction, let the children lead us.
While they know no disillusionment, let the children love us,
  that we may be healed,
  that we may trust again . . .
  that we may regain our faith . . .
  that we may recover our innocence . . .
  that we may become children of the Father of Life.

7
Forgive us all for the damage we've done

Lord, forgive us all for the damage we've done to our world,
    to Your world.

So many are suffering from our ignorance and carelessness.

Cancer is epidemic from the toxins we eat and breathe.

Animals are disappearing from their natural habitats
      as we cover the grasses with concrete
         and trade forests for mega-marts.

The foods are often unsafe because of the wastes we've emptied
    into the waters
        and chemicals we've spread on our soils
            and additives we've fed to farm animals.
We know that the designer diseases
    for which there seem to be no cures
        are consequences of many bad choices.
May we learn from our mistakes and seek Your solutions.
Lead us to cures that You have built into this marvelous creation
    in Your characteristic grace.
May we teach our children reverence
    for the delicate balance You intended between us
        and the rest of creation.
Teach us the art of redemption.
May we mend the brokenness within our reach
    by Your touch of grace.

8
The world
is in turmoil

The world is in turmoil.

Bewilderment and confusion at the deepest level

  fulfill the ancient prediction

  black will be white—

  wrong will be right.

Absolute truths have been made relative . . .

Even the Golden Rule has been tarnished—altered to read:

  "Do to others what You think they would do to You

  if they had the chance."

Goodness seems to always have an angle.

Manipulate-your-way-to-the-top lessons begin in daycare.

Theology is twisted to create more loopholes—
    true righteousness is the object of scorn,
        even in ecclesiastical circles.
The questions children ask are answered with cynicism.
Innocence is destroyed before it can have a chance to root
    and sprout into virtue.
Build an ark, Lord.
Call some crazy Noah for our day.
Find with Your perfect vision someone who will saw wood
    (when it has never rained) to build a great ship.
Rescue a remnant of trust—
    a fragment of faith.
And, Lord, if even the jackass was invited
    to bring a mate and start anew,
        could You choose—could You use me?

9
We thought
we needed more
information

We thought we needed more information.
We thought that we would make better decisions
    if we knew more.
The apple offered control of our lives . . .
    of other lives.
If we just had the apple, our own personal apple,
    no one, not even God, could tell us what to do.
So we got the information;
    we drove at breakneck speed
    through the information highway.

We raced through the orchard, making a network of brickyards
    between apple trees.
Now we have information.
We sit so immobilized by so much information
    that we can no longer make choices—
We have no way to weigh so much information.
Dazed and intoxicated by the glut, we are paralyzed to act,
    to feel, to move.
The apple juice drips from our chins
    as we stare blankly at images of each other,
        images we can manipulate and alter on the screen.
Oh, Lord, we have too much information!
And we have lost—with our innocence—our wisdom,
    our outrage
        our delight . . .
            our Eden.

10
Thank You
for making
peace portable

Thank You, Lord, for making peace portable.
Here in the city there are only man-made surroundings—
    structures, highways, sidewalks.
Here in the center city mall
    there has never been silence
        since the first jackhammer
            pounded through old concrete
                to make a place to pour the new.

Music we can't identify is only the pulse
    of a great beating heart—the city.
        It has no tune.
            There is no harmony—
                There is only the beat.
But You are here, Lord.
It is Your robe we brush as we pass in the crush of rush hour.
Turn to us, Lord.
Ask again: "Who touched Me?"
For even here we can draw virtue from You
    if we can just touch the hem of Your garment.
Your Spirit is peace.
    "Peace—be still."
Whisper to the waves of humanity.
    Speak to the winds of change.
        Still the tides of public opinion.
If You speak, there is a center of peace.
If we touch Your hem, we are made whole—
    our broken parts are mended—
        we are pulled back together.
Even here—in the city—peace in the storm.

11
There is water
in the basement

There is water in the basement this morning, Lord.
The avalanche of snow we've been accumulating
    has begun to melt.
The rains have pounded the frozen ground
    while ice still clogs the ditches and the drains.
The water oozed in under the basement door—
    it seeped through the walls and the cracks—
        through our waterproof paint
           through the cement
               through the carpet.
The ground was so saturated
    with water from the swollen underground springs,
        so covered with water from the saturated clouds
           that there was nowhere for the water to go
               but into our sealed-in spaces,
               into our dry walls,
               through the tiny cracks and crevices.

Lord, in these last days You promised rains of the Spirit.

You promised to open the heavens and pour out such a deluge
that earth would not contain it.

We've built some pretty airtight spaces, Lord.

We've coated our souls with skepticism
and covered our hearts with lethargy.

We've built walls of suspicion and protected
our tender inner places with sophisticated cynicism
lest we be invaded and taken advantage of by charlatans.

We are dry, Lord, and our dryness has caused
cracks to form in our defenses.

Rain on us. Soak the frozen arid land
with Your Spirit.

Saturate the ground of our being
with the living waters—
from springs below—
from clouds above,
invade our sealed-off souls.

Seep into our corners and through our crevices.

Sweep in through the doors.

Pound the window wells with insistent yearning.

Lord, when Your rains come,
let it be more than a mist; we need a flood!

Rain on us.

12
Sometimes
I can't sleep

Sometimes I can't sleep, Lord.

At night everything looms large before my mind.

At night the issues of the day organize themselves into an army,
    marching like an enemy advancing
        to pillage my storehouse of peace.

Worries and concerns of the day turn into terrors of the night.

Simple shortcomings and human frailties become terminal failures
    for which there is no grace or mercy.

I feel as if I am slipping off a precipice
    and the sapling I grasp
        is coming up by the roots.

I am alone and a stalker lurches in the shadows.

I know, Lord, that You are not the author of confusion.

You are never the source of fear,

for fear is the opposite of faith;

I recognize the terror of the night

as the imposition of Satan.

So, I've made Satan a promise:

If he awakens me in the night,

I will spend every sleepless moment praying.

I will pray for my children;

I will intercede for the lost;

I will lift up my husband to the Father.

I will plead for the salvation of our neighborhood,

our country, our world.

I will pledge with the psalmist to spend every waking hour

"remembering You on my bed."

I will "meditate on You in the night watches."

Since I made this promise I find I win

either way:

If I am awake, I have sweet communion with You, Lord.

Or I doze into peaceful rest. Selah!

13
Thank You
for friends

Thank You, Lord, for friends.

Through the passages of life, good friends remain.

Through beauty and vitality

    through the loss of energy and elasticity,

    through stellar achievement

    and through embarrassing failure—friends remain.

Friends give when there is need—

They celebrate and enjoy with us

    when there is abundance.

They laugh at our jokes and our foibles.

They cry at our griefs and at our sadnesses.

Friends pick up the pieces we leave,

>they take up the slack when we're careless

>and they make up the difference when we come up short.

They listen when we tell them something . . .

>. . . and they hear when we don't.

They love our kids, tolerate our dogs and accept our spouses.

Lord, of all the sweet relationships of earth,

>thank You for the gift of a few good friends.

And, most of all, thank You for choosing to be One to us

>who were and are so in need of one True Friend.

14
O God, Creator
of all that is

O God, Creator of all that is,
I revel in the elements,
  embrace the big parts of Your handiwork!
The oceans.
The wide expanse of oceans that toss and rage—
  restless, ceaseless, fathomless;
    like gushes of amniotic fluids,
      the waters nurture, birthing life-forms below,
        seeding the clouds above,
        feeding the land beings—
          all from their mysterious store.

The winds.

The winds with their many personalities—

    —the coy spring breezes

    —the scorching desert winds

    —the straight winds that blast with hurricane force

    —the whirling twisters that churn into their
        vortexes the edifices of man and prune the
        branches of trees

    —the playful kite winds of summer,
        chasing and tugging children
        across summer meadows

    —the winds that bring rain, banish clouds and promise snow.

The earth.

The raw earth in all its elemental forms—

    —red clay and black loam,

    —coarse rocks and powdery sand

    —boulders and caverns of gray, onyx,
        pink and rust-colored stone.

        —the plowed pregnant soil of Midwest farmland,

        —the prairie dirt sprouting a hundred native grasses

        —the rich forest floor of decaying plant life
            nurturing the newly fallen seeds of the passing species.

I celebrate fire—

　　—the intimidating fire of flashing lightning,

　　—the small smolder of a curled dry leaf

　　　　ignited by the sunlight on a glistening rock crystal.

　　—the rage of forest fire

　　　　purging the undergrowth,

　　　　preparing the habitat for jack pine and brown thrush

　　　　and all those amazing life forms

　　　　　　that only grow

　　　　　　in fire-purged places.

And, Lord, while I'm glad You made the small things,

　　　　the microscopic detail—thank You for the big stuff—

　　　　　　those things that dwarf me and put all else into perspective.

Thank You for the awesome—

　　for the seas

　　　　and the wind

　　　　　　earth and fire.

　　　　　　　　Thank You for the elemental!

15
There is a ship
on the horizon

There is a ship on the horizon,
    sails at full mast,
        moving steadily
            with the strong and pleasant winds.
Lord, I am earthbound here,
    and I can only watch the great ship,
        lifted by the sea,
            carried by the wind,
                moving with the currents.
How I long, Jesus, to hoist anchor—
    let loose of my earth attachments—
        and sail with the Experienced Captain
            over boundless sea.

How I long to be moved by the winds of the Spirit,
    to follow the currents of Your grace.
You, too, loved the sea.
No wonder You taught with so many metaphors of sailing!
No wonder the whole faith adventure is away from land,
    buoyed on the waves,
        safe only in the ark.
No wonder we must bury our earth-life
    and all its entanglements under the waters of baptism,
    then emerge into new life, leaving our old earth-lives
        at the bottom of the sea.
It is in the ark of salvation that we are at rest,
    even when storms rage.
It is the "sealing,"
    the "covering" of Your atonement
        that makes the ark impervious to the raging tempests.
And it is You, Yourself,
    who will sail us to the greening New World
        where we will disembark
            to play like innocents
                on the shore of the sparkling sea.

16
These words are ineffective today

Oh Jesus, these words are ineffective today.

They float like dead leaves on the surface of the river.

But my prayer is in the depths;

my prayer is drowning on the bottom.

Hardly a bubble of living breath is reaching the surface.

So, God, articulation is out of the question.

Were Your words true
    when You promised to articulate for us at times like this?
Can the Spirit actually turn my throat-wrenching groans
    into something You can hear?
Can Your great heart reverberate
    to the quivering vibrations of my panicked heart?
Because one thing is certain:
    my groanings cannot be uttered.
The circumstances won't allow them to be.
    And I can't translate this pain into words anyway.
        I groan.
Like an injured animal my spirit groans.
Can You take my raw groanings and make a prayer of them?

17
I get so oblivious
to the wonders

Lord, I get so oblivious to the wonders in my life.
I eat food but forget to relish the delicate subtleties of tastes—
I travel the country so often and so far
    that I find myself much more attentive
        to the time it takes to reach my destination
            than the rich colors of the countryside,
            the miracle of the changing seasons,
        the warm breezes that carry the fragrances
            of damp soil,
            fresh grasses, budding fruit trees,
            or newly cut hay at harvest time.
I fall into bed at night
    going over what I managed to get done today
        when I should be thanking You
            for a set of crisp sheets, a good bed,
                clean quilts and the body of the man
                I love at rest beside me.

Come morning, I hit the floor running, gulp a cup of coffee
and a slice of toast.
But seldom do I rejoice in the joy of being able to walk,
run, skip, climb,
go and do.
I am surrounded by treasured relationships.
Not often enough do I stop
to really look into the faces of those I love so much
and have a party in my heart in celebration
of their beauty, uniqueness, variety
and wonderful humor
that makes me laugh, enjoy
and sometimes endure.
So, Lord, I'm asking You to make me aware of this day's gifts.
May I live in constant awe and gratitude.
Today I would see, taste, smell, touch, hear . . .
and be fully alive!

18
I watch the children on the carousel

I watch the children on the carousel this morning, Lord.
They are mesmerized by the glittering horses,
   the bejeweled elephants,
      the undulating lights.
The merry-go-round starts to turn as the music plays,
   and, one by one,
      the images familiar:
         mother, father, tables, cars, grass—
            blending into a spinning blur—
               disappear.
The children gradually come to embrace a new reality,
   the world of bright, flawless animals,
      colored lights, music box sounds.

Only peers populate their brave new world.
Their wide eyes become fixed
on the mechanized, artificial wonder—
blind to any other reality.
Lord, am I, too, spinning in my artificial world,
caught up in glittering plans,
dazzled by artifacts of our culture?
Are my ears so tuned to the tinny sounds
that fill my hearing, that sweet voices of those I love
can no longer be distinguished from the din?
Has the centrifugal force of my running-around-in-circles
blurred Your dear face into oblivion?
Is my whole perception of reality
based on the habits and lifestyles of those who spin with me?
Slow me down, Lord.
Let my contrived machinery run out of steam.
Let the music stop.
Pull me out of my trance.
Let the light bulbs go out;
let the sunshine stream in!

Blow Your clean, fresh breezes into my stupored face.
Give me a hand, Lord.
Lift me from the phony conveyances
    and set my feet on solid ground.
I may be disoriented for a while, Lord.
    Steady me with Your strong arm.

I may be blinded by the bright light of Your truth at first.
Be patient with me
    until I can refocus on the images
        You want to reveal to me.
Lord, lead me into a quiet place
    where I can learn to hear the gentle sound
        of the clear brooks of Living Water.
And, when I can bear it,
    let me hear Your voice—
    let me see Your face.
    Let me walk in Your paths.
    Let me recognize the eternal in every fragile moment.

19
We've been driving through the mountains

We've been driving through the mountains, Lord—
    winding our way in an air-conditioned car up the narrow road
      cutting through the towering oaks and maples,
        pines and tulip trees.
The mountain laurel and sassafras sprouts
    are at eye level as we drive along
      and I know the fragrance is heavenly
        mixed with the musky smells of mosses and rich earth.
Why was I so timid, then, Lord,
    when I suggested we roll down all the windows?
Why was I so easily silenced
    when someone said the wind would mess up our hair?
Now, I know we will return to the flat plains with our hair intact,
    but not our spirits.

The mountain trails were beautiful to behold,
   but You gave us at least five senses
      as avenues to transport food to our souls,
         and we settled for using only sight.
We could have filled our nostrils with fresh mountain air
   fragrant with a hundred rare perfumes.
We could have heard the leathery rhythm band
   of colliding oak leaves accompanying
      the song of a thousand birds.
We could have felt the wind in our hair, caressing our faces.
We could have stopped
   and touched the shagbark hickories
      and the smooth beeches.
We could have pulled up a small sassafras seedling
   and nibbled on a sliver of root.
We could have peeked under a tulip leaf
   to find the lovely yellow and orange blossom
      so rare to huge trees.
We might have stopped at one of the pull-off places
   and leaned over a cliff to see the valley below
      and beheld vistas that would have taken our breath away.
But at least, Lord, we didn't sweat
   and our hair didn't get messed up.

20
We need to choose roads we can trust

Lord, we need to choose roads we can trust
    to take us to right destinations.
The road sign here says "Old Burnt Mill Road."
This road leads not to a promise,
    but to a tragic disappointment—
        to a place that no longer exists.
One could walk miles down this road
    and only come to the charred remains
        of somebody else's dreams.
Yesterday the sign I passed simply said "Dead End";
    and sometimes there isn't even a warning.

The sign says "Old State Road 3,"
     but when the state opened the bypass,
          they just put up a guard rail across the old pavement.
Now the road just stops—
     a promise of a journey
          that turns out to take us nowhere.
Thank You, Lord, for Your road signs,
     for they are always accurate.
"The way of the transgressor is hard."
"He who will endure to the end will be saved."
"Narrow is the gate and straight the way
     that leads to eternal life."
"Trust in the Lord and He shall direct Your paths."
You always tell us right up front exactly
     where life's paths will take us.
Thank You, most of all, for making it simple.
"I am the Way, the Truth, and the Life," You said.
If I want all the best destinations,
     I just have to choose You.
That road will take me home.

21
I walked down
to the water

I walked down to the water this morning, Lord.
I wanted to hear from You,
 to be near the silent rocks,
  to hear whispering ripples
   of the morning bayside.
As I sat in the sand,
 my eye caught some faint writing on a flat rock.
I held the stone at an angle
 so I could read what someone had scratched there:
  "For all who lost what they never found."
Who put that message on the stone?

What had they lost themselves
	to identify with such lostness?
		a lover?
			a child?
				a vision?
					an opportunity?
					a dream?
The stone was heavy, Lord;
	not the kind that could be tossed aside—
		not a pebble to be skipped across the surface of the lake.
Your life on this earth wrote a different message—
	You, the stone hewed out of the mountain,
		You, the Stone the builders rejected
			that became the Chief Cornerstone.
On that stone God wrote,
	"For those who find what they can never lose."
On one stone is despair.
	On the other, hope.
Thank You for the hope we can build upon.

22
Sometimes I feel guilty for being still

Lord, sometimes I feel guilty for being still.

My soul feels small and shriveled;

    I know I need to stop—

    I need to center my mind, my emotions, my plans

        on You.

Yet, when I save time to be quiet before You,

    when I stop the motion and find a place to listen,

        I feel guilty.

I have been too conditioned to gauge my worth

    by what I am getting done,

        instead of on what You have already done.

Lord, this pressure to accomplish something
     is felt even more in those circles
          where Your name is used freely.
"What are You doing for the Lord?"
     seems to be the important question—
          spoken and implied.
But my spirit tells me that these are human expectations,
     not divine ones.
What You want is relationship with me.
Lord, I am here today to enjoy You,
     to be with You,
          listen to You.
Would You take me into Your presence
     and wash away the earth from my feet
          so that I may walk into Your place
               without leaving dirty prints on Your carpets?
Let me be at rest in the silence.
I bring nothing—
     except my hunger and my full attention.

23
Will starts
to school today

Will starts to school today, Lord—
    his first day of first grade.
He is so innocent and so ready to learn.
But what he may learn could chip away at his character
    and erode his belief in You and in himself.
My impulse is to protect him—
    that's the grandmother in me.

But save me from letting the "protection instinct" take the form
of cocooning him from those experiences
that could build his character
and develop his moral muscle.
Let my "protection" take the form of prayer
so that You can equip him with the whole armor of faith—
a faith forged through experience and choices
and not through withdrawal and fear.
Remind me of ways to make Your Word a part of his days.
Show me ways to make his real life
an object lesson for Your wisdom.
May I show him joy!
Let the breastplate of right living
be a joyous thing for him to remember
as he leaves our family circle to enter the world.
And may the warmth of love, forgiveness and grace
draw him always back home.
Lord, I give You Will today.
You promised: "I, Myself, the Lord God, will shepherd My sheep."
Count Will in on that, would You?

24
The second plane
behind us

Lord, the second plane behind us made a crash landing.
There was a strong tailwind and when the pilot
    broke through the low ceiling
        so close to the ground,
           the plane met the runway too quickly.
He pointed the nose down so as not to land too far down the runway
    and prevent running out of the landing space,
        but the plane touched down too hard
           and bent the landing gear.

Now the sirens are screeching
　　and the lights are flashing
　　　　and no planes can get in.
They circle somewhere up above the cloud cover,
　　but no one can land.
Lord, I, too, am an inexperienced pilot of a small craft.
My miscalculations can sometimes be tragic,
　　not only to myself but to others whose progress
　　　　I impede when I mess up.
But You have equipped my craft with instruments
　　to receive Your signals.
　　　　Keep me alert to them.
　　　　Don't let me trust my own instincts,
　　　　　　which are not trustworthy.
You are the strong tower.
You are the Master of the winds.
I will fly into the unknown with confidence
　　only if I can keep a clear channel to Your heart.
"Though I ride the morning winds
　　to the far corners of the sky,
　　　　even there Your hand will guide me,
　　　　　　Your strength will support me."

25
Thank You for the sermons of the sea

Thank You, Lord, for the sermons of the sea.
After a beautiful clear day of warm sunshine and shell scavenging,
   the mists began to roll in.
Like smoke from a bonfire,
   the fog began to creep over the dune grasses and over the beach.
By evening the gray houses were disappearing
   along with the sea pines, scrub oaks and bayberry bushes.
All that remained were dim shadowy ghosts of objects;
   even the ocean was gone from sight
      and the sunset was lost somewhere in the gray.

If I had been a stranger to this island, just arriving,
    if I were to trust my sight,
        it would have been easy to doubt
            that there were houses all around.
Someone could tell me about the ocean,
    seashells and the glorious sunsets.
I might have said, "It's alright for you to believe in all those things;
    I'm glad you find them true for you, but I'm a realist."
Lord, this morning it is clear again.
As I walk the road of the spirit today,
    let me hold to Your truth,
        to the clear revelations You've given me
            all back along my path.
And, when the mists of gray move in,
    remind me that clouds are not the substance of life;
        they only veil it for a moment.

26
Our church has started a "banner" ministry

Lord, our church has started a "banner" ministry.
I guess You know about banners
    because You mention them in Your Word.
I especially like the verse where You say
    that Your banner over me is love.
Lord, the banners help us worship You.
They are full of deep and meaningful symbols that remind us
    of Your attributes and qualities and character:
        the lamb, the crown, the water of life,
            the alpha and omega, the lamp, the bread.

The symbols remind us of what You do:
broken chains, open prison cells, water in the desert,
a shepherd's staff, manna, the cross.
Today when we entered the sanctuary
there were green banners
neatly and symmetrically hung
down both sides of the aisles.
These banners were empty—
no symbols, no braid, no glitter, no message—
just identical strips of felt
cut in a "V" at the bottom edge and hung from poles.
They picked up the same deep color of the artificial ferns
that had been placed along the ledge
under the white panels that hide the audio speakers.
The contrast of the green with the church's off-white interior
was lovely and coordinated.
The decor was pleasing to the eye.
But there was no message.
There was nothing to disturb our reverie,
nothing to provoke our minds or challenge our assumptions.
Nothing to reveal any insights into Your nature—
or ours.

Lord, is there a message from You in all this?

Are we all soldiers carrying a banner through this world
    reflecting and depicting some aspect of Your nature?

Does the world gain insights into who You are
    by the banners we carry
    and by the way Your soldiers march in relationship
        with each other?

Have we opted for pleasant decor
    instead of challenging revelations?

Are Your metaphors too much work for us to define
    when fellow sojourners puzzle over Your mysteries?

Lord, I don't want to march around today
    with a blank flag flapping in the breeze.

Emblazon something amazing on the banner of my life.

Use me to declare some truth that could cause an army to march
    or a nation to be born
        or a revolution to explode.

27
Just as the day slips off the western horizon

Just as the day slips off the western horizon, Lord,
   I slip off to steal a moment of solitude.
No, maybe a "moment of companionship" is more accurate.
I've been with everyone else today, Lord:
   my children, their children, my husband,
      my fellow workers, my friends, a few strangers.
But all the while, like a girl with her lover on her consciousness,

You have hovered on the edges of my mind.
I could feel You there being patient,
    being present.
But it isn't enough for You to be present to me;
    I want to be present to You.
I thank You for all the relationships in my life.
It is You that has made them beautiful.
But You Yourself are the dearest of all.
    You are the Lover of my soul.
Now, as the sun sinks behind the trees
    leaving its scarlet and gold reflections on the water,
        it seems I can feel You whispering
            in the rising evening breeze:
                "Arise, My love, and come away . . ."
                I arise, my Lord, and follow.

28
It's morning and my senses are rested

It's morning, my Lord, and my senses are rested
    from yesterday's assault of stimulation.
This morning I am aware of the delicious regularness of this day:
        the clean, cool sheets smooth against my skin,
    the fragrant familiarness of this house,
    the sound of my husband's much-loved body breathing beside me,
    the white pine branch brushing against the window,
    the children who are talking and giggling upstairs
        in their parents' childhood bedrooms.

Help me to savor the simplicity of today,
   to hold each tasty morsel on my tongue
      and enjoy its gift before I swallow it into the process of my life.
Lord, I would live sacramentally.
"This is My body . . ."
   I hold this moment of Your life, and give transforming thanks.
May these simple elements be changed
   into Your very Self as I partake of them.
May the lifeblood of this scarlet morning move through my veins
   making me a part of this day . . . and of You.
I raise my chalice and toast the dawn.
   "Do this is remembrance . . ."

29
I love these little cafés in the morning

Lord, I love these little cafés in the morning.
All over the world they're the same:
   small, chatty pockets of community
      clustered around formica-top tables
        discussing the farm prices,
          the pecking order at the factory,
          road conditions,
            some neighbor's kids,
              or the local election.
Scattered in the room are people alone who have come
   to absorb the noise and fellowship
      they miss so much
        since a spouse died or ran off with some younger love,
        or they moved here to start a new career in a new place.

The waitresses are always blunt and sassy—
　　just like your mother or your aunt Mandy—
　　　　keeping a jovial familiarity that feels like home,
　　　　　　even if you've never had one.
And the waitress does everything like Mom did:
　　takes the orders, keeps the coffee brewing,
　　clears off used dishes,
　　wipes tables and counter tops with a white rag with red edging
　　and sweeps up crumbs under the toddler's high chair.
Lord, sometimes I wonder what would happen
　　if these people here in the café this morning
　　　　were all the people left to start a new world.
How many days would it take for leaders to emerge,
　　for talents to be assigned to certain tasks,
　　　　for a government of sorts with rules
　　　　　　and boundaries to be formed,
　　　　for entertainers to step forward to oil the system
　　　　　　with laughter and lightness
　　　　　　　　when things became hard and heavy?
Who would call this new society to worship
　　and remind us all of our insufficiency,
　　　　and that without the Spirit we would become animals
　　　　　　and devour one another.

The ark must have been a bit like a café.
It started out as a group of people related to Noah
and pulled together by a disaster
into the shelter of a safe haven.
But once the flood was over
and the earth was left to sprout again
and the animals were busy propagating,
unlikely assignments must have called undeveloped
abilities and talents out of these individuals.
And the great demands of a new society
must have exposed latent flaws in their character, too.
Lord, in any world, on any day,
we human beings carry with us
the seed of the divine and the root of sin.
Today, remind me of my potential to be a saint or a fiend,
an apostle or an infidel.
In the society I move in today,
may I embrace the life of the Spirit and lean heavily on You.
Deliver me from the choices of my baser nature
and give me a revelation of Your government, Your family,
Your Holy Nation.
May Thy Kingdom come,
Thy will be done on earth—today—as it is in heaven.
So what is my assignment?
Amen.

30
Thinking about the young African-American policeman

Lord, I keep thinking
    about the young African-American policeman
        who was on the news this morning.
His face haunts me—the pain of betrayal I saw there.
Lord, how could his fellow officers be so cruel and insensitive
    as to all dress up in Ku Klux Klan's hoods of hatred
        and surround and taunt him—
            people he trusted, people he worked with?
Why did they think that was a funny joke,
    that he should laugh afterward and have his picture taken
        with them in their horrible costumes?

Lord, why do we, how do we,
    devise such ugly ways to hurt
        each other?
After all these centuries of pain and war and bigotry,
    it seems that we would learn,
        yet it seems the depths of our deprivation sinks lower.
At the next table, Lord, is a beautiful curly-headed little boy
    having his lunch with his mother and young grandmother.
He delights in everything: the food he is trying,
    the egret on the sidewalk waiting for crumbs,
        me—a stranger at the next table.
Protect his innocence as long as possible, Lord.
Delay the influences of a fallen world.
Yet I know the day will come when he, too,
    will make a choice that is hurtful and with that choice
        Eden's drama will be played out again.
Cover that baby, and the man on the news
    and those men who taunted him
        with the shadow of the cross.
Without You, we all are Judas and Herod and Hitler.
With You, we are children again, children of the King.
"Come into our hearts, Lord Jesus . . ."
    Amen.

31
How thankful I am for the morning

How thankful I am, Lord, for the morning!
With sleep, without sleep, morning is hope.
When nights are peaceful
 and sleep can restore the body and the soul,
  morning is a new opportunity.
Morning is new energy,
 new enlightenment,
  new inspiration.
When nights are restless, plagued by phantoms of doubt and fear,
 morning is a clearing in the deep dark forest.

It is the sorting-out time,
   the grappling-with-issues time—
      the time to "do something about it."
No wonder, Lord, Your Word so often refers to heaven and eternity,
   as the "morning," the "dawning,"
      the "endless day" where You are the Light.
In a way, all of life here is a night of sorts,
   and for most of us that night is a restless, worried night.
But You have promised us the dawn and in that morning
   there will never be another sleepless night.
That morning will be better than "hope,"
   for hope is for things unseen, unrealized as yet.
But in Your new day, reality will replace and eclipse
   all our finest hopes.
Thank You, Lord.
   Thank You for morning!

32
You know I have always wanted to sing

Lord, You know I have always wanted to sing—
    to have a voice so sweet and tender
        that it could communicate to hardened and broken hearts
           the gentle healing in Your Good News.
I have struggled with my limitations,
    been frustrated with writing songs I couldn't myself sing.
But You are teaching me, Lord,
    that it is the song of my heart that You hear,
        and You are the only audience.
If my soul sings to You,
    You will put the song in the places it needs to go.
You alone can convince and You alone can restore.
Only You can repair and make new.
It is Your song that first fills me before my heart can sing.
When my voice is inadequate and weak,
    drown it out with the song of my soul.

33
You are teaching me the importance of finishing the race

Lord, You are teaching me the importance of finishing the race.
I've never dwelt much on sports metaphors;
    I'm not much of an athlete.
I'm so thankful You didn't say "win the race,"
    but You did say "finish."
Lord, life is full of times it would be easier to drop out,
    to be the runner left behind,
        injured or exhausted at the side of the road
            while the surviving pack leaves me to eat their dust.

But this race is not a sprint;

it is a marathon with varied terrain and twists in the trail.

The point is to finish.

How encouraging it is to know that the great apostle Paul

summed up his life, not in terms of "winning,"

but of finishing the course, endurance.

What victory for me in Your words from the cross—

the last words before the resurrection: "It is finished!"

Today, Lord, I may be quick.

I may find this mile of the journey easy for me.

Tomorrow the course may be uphill or through hairpin turns.

I may turn my ankle on a rock or stumble.

I may lose speed or pick up the pace.

But, with Your coaching and Your care, I will finish the race.

I've gone too far to drop out now.

34
Where could
I go from
Your presence?

"Where could I go from Your presence, Lord?" is more
    than a rhetorical question these days.
Where my journey has taken me
    has been something I could never have plotted or planned.
No road club could have printed out maps for this trip.
Yet, I never left the palm of Your hand.

Now, more than ever, I am at rest in Your sweet embrace.

How can this be?

Turbulent times should be unsettling.

Strange territory should leave us

feeling bewildered and disoriented.

Yet here I am—somehow at rest in Your presence.

That is familiar, reassuring, peaceful.

The psalmist must have learned this, too.

I can never be lost from Your presence.

If I go down to hell, Your presence surrounds me

like a safe harbor.

If I fly through the heavens on the wings of the morning,

Your sweet presence puts music to the words.

You are the eye of the storm.

You are the cleft in the rock.

You are the whale in the bottom of the sea.

I've never been here before, Lord, but I know where I am.

I am with You.

35
This island
is the arsenal
of memories

Lord, this island is the arsenal of memories for our family.
 Good joy-filled days of summer,
  melancholy days of autumn,
  passages of our lives,
  stages of our children,
  chapters of friendship—
   these have been marked and celebrated,
   closed and mourned,
    recalled and revisited here.

This year, the theme song of my heart is gratitude.

I am thankful for it all and for the years and experiences
    that have given me perspective on it all.

Islands—especially this one with so much history of its own—
    give me perspective.

Islands are apart, separated by space, sea and refreshing breezes,
    from the network of mainland demands.

From islands a sense of priority emerges—
    an overview of all that pushes and shoves us around
        on pressured days.

Thank You, Lord, for islands and for this one in particular.
    Teach me.
        Show me.

I thank You for all I see from here today.

36
It is so easy to take things into our own hands

Lord, it is so easy to take things into our own hands,
  get ahead of Your timing, mess things up.
How impatient I am!
How arrogant sometimes—
  thinking I can bring about justice,
  hoping I can precipitate heart change,
  believing that I can hasten the coming of Your kingdom
    in the souls of other people.
Let me learn from the river, Lord.
  Day by day,
    year by year,
      decade by decade it flows to the sea.

No matter what men do to try
     to change the course
     to accommodate and facilitate their self-serving purposes,
          the river persistently, consistently responds
               to the magnet of the great waters.
It seeks its own destination from a source deep
     in the bedrock of the planet.
For a while men and engineering genius can reroute the river—
     but rise the high floods,
          descend the drought years,
               the river from its deep source re-carves its path
                    to the sea, to the arms of the embracing sea.
And in its pure and unquenchable thirst for the sea,
     its current carves through any obstacle in its path.
Mountains are dissected; plains are traversed,
     valleys are created.
In the natural course of its mission, the river serves.
It carries rich soil to the riverbed farmlands.
It makes a way of transportation across flat stretches of prairie.
It irrigates strips of food-producing and life-sustaining land
     in the midst of the desert.

Fish thrive in its cool moving waters.

Birds and wildlife grow fat along its banks.

But all these things are only *results*,

    never for the river's own purpose.

The driving force is just the simple and powerful pull of the sea.

Lord, I want to seek You.

Let the passion of my life be to lose myself in You.

Let the deep desire that springs from the bedrock of my being

    be to flow to You.

Keep me unaware of any result

    except the deep peace of knowing

        that part of my spirit has already reached

            its destination and is at rest in You.

May the journey of my life cut its way through any obstacle

    for the insatiable hunger to empty myself

        into the great sea of Yourself.

        You—the Source.

        You—the destination.

Whatever else may happen today, let it only and always

    be the natural result of a river, flowing to the sea.

        Amen. And amen.

37
My friend
is depleted

Lord, my friend is depleted.
The day-after-day demands of caring for the man she loves
    as his health seems to crumble in her hands
        is sucking her dry.
Small victories, huge defeats;
    encouraging moments,
        discouraging days
            see-saw over the arched frame of her optimism.
But gradually the weight added
    to both ends of the teeter-totter
        has begun to cut deep into her spirit.
Hold her up, Lord.

Help me today to know how I can ease the load,
    maybe give perspective to what comes to feel like
        a win/lose situation.
Lord, some days it looks like a lose/lose prospect.
But we both know—and her husband, my dear friend, also knows—
    that under it all it's really a win/win situation.
Lord, death is not the problem.
    It's the daily grinding away of the dying process
        that wears our spirits raw.
Let friendship be a healing balm today.
    Let us laugh; laughter heals.
    Let us cry; tears bathe the wound.
    Let us have good conversations about
        children, politics, travel, work, writing and speaking—
            good conversation about the stuff of life
                that diverts our attention.
    Let us reminisce; memory gives perspective on the present.
    Let us pray; prayer teaches us to relinquish control
        to the only One who knows where we're all going
        and how we should get there.
Lord, thank You for my friend.
Heal her spirit today;
    let me be the one to nurse her to wellness today.
        Come, Healer of Spirits. Make us whole again.

38
Thank You

Lord, thank You.

Today I am just grateful.

Thankful that after the roller coaster of life,

I still have a husband who loves me

and whom I love with an intensity

neither of us were capable of as young lovers.

I'm thankful we're together—

so many of our friends are not with their mates—

and love sharing the beauty of life.

I'm thankful, Lord, for tastes,

especially here in this faraway port

where pasta is an art

and sauces are a creation of the soul.

I'm thankful for the sight I enjoyed—
   the picture printed on my mind
      of little narrow row houses
         of yellow, peach, cream and blue
            lining the azure harbor,
   the bay filled with white boats and sailing vessels,
      the blue and green awninged cafés
         inviting us to stop and absorb the marvel.
I'm thankful for the smells of cheese and marinara,
   cappuccino and chocolate,
      olive oil and basil—
         their tastes laced with those of homemade bread,
            fresh pasta and Italian ices.
Thank You, Lord, for friends—
   for good conversation and a sympathetic ear;
      for a shared love of art, poetry and music!
Thank You for a foundation of years shared, lessons learned,
   joys celebrated, children raised,
      meals served, and nights of love and rest.

39
The gift I bring
You today

The gift I bring You today, Lord
    is not easy for me to give.
Oh, not because I don't want You to have it.
    I do.
But because it is in pieces and scattered all over my life.
If it were in one neat chunk, it would be easy.
But at this point, I'm quite sure I can't even find them all—
    and some pieces are such strange shapes
        I'm not sure I'd even recognize them to give You.
So I'm giving You the pieces I see and recognize,
    the ones I can identify.
And I'm giving You my pledge:
    If You'll help me find the rest of the pieces—
        no matter how long it takes

or how deeply embedded they are

    in the fabric of my days—

        I will give You those, too.

Is that something You'll accept?

It's sort of a gift on the installment plan, I guess.

    And like an installment, You own it and have it coming.

Please search my heart

    and know that it is my true desire

        to give You all of it.

My gift to You, Jesus, is control.

Save me from the influence of a world, a time and a culture

    that brainwash me daily in every way

        to believe that being in control,

            taking control,

                and never losing control

                    is the only way to live.

I know that instead it is the quickest way to die.

    It is the Eden story all over again.

Today, Lord, take control of my life.

    I give You all the control I can find.

        Help me find it all and give it with joy.

        Amen.

40
There was a time when I was happy

There was a time, Lord, when I was happy,
    but pain had not plumbed my happiness deep enough
        to be truthfully called joy.
There was a time when I knew and celebrated
    true things,
        but experience had not yet sent me
            over perilous pilgrimages
                in pursuit of a Holy Grail.
There was a time when I made eager plans
    for a future,
        but I had not yet learned
            to embrace eternity in the moments I had.
Thank You, Lord, for the road I've traveled.
Only now am I discovering
    that it is beautiful to praise God in all things.
Today, at least, I do.
Praise You.
Amen.

41
Help me not focus so much on the distance

Lord, help me not focus so much
    on the distance I have yet to go.
Let me today only be thankful for the miles I've covered,
    the distances run.
Lord, Paul said we should keep our eyes on the goal.
I guess that's true enough.
We shouldn't get distracted by obstacles or sore muscles
    and give up.
But for me the goal looks so unattainable,
    so far away.
When I am hurting from the journey,
    the goal seems to remind me
        that I'm not as good at this as I hoped I would be.

But it helps me most to enjoy the beauty of where I am.
It helps to see the child playing in the sand,
    to watch for dolphins jumping
        or pelicans swooping
            or the amazing piece of sand dollar
                a foot or two in front of me.
When I enjoy the journey,
    when I smile at fellow runners
        and read their T-shirts,
            try to guess what their lives are all about—
    when I step aside to let someone else pass
        or exchange treasures that we've found—
            then, before I know it,
I find when I look up,
    that the goal is so much closer
        and I have my second wind.
Today, Lord, I will ever keep in mind the goal.
But I will also rejoice over the distance run
    and delight in the journey.
        Amen.

42
I've heard and read all my life that You are light

Lord, I've heard and read all my life that You are light.

The songs, poems, sermons, books and articles about light
have almost become cliché.

I've heard it said You are a light for my path,

and that the light will only shine on the very next step,

so we must walk one step at a time.

I've heard You compared to a candle,

a dim light that only looks bright when it is in utter darkness;

then it shows up,

becomes dramatic by comparison.

But Revelation says in heaven

there is no need for the sun or the moon

because You are the light.

That doesn't sound like a flashlight or a candle to me!

Your Word also says that You *are* the light

and in You there is no darkness at all!

Today at the ocean there is not a cloud in the sky.

The light is so pristine that everything

is illuminated in all its beauty.

Colors are radiant!

The water is azure!

The flowers are outrageously brilliant!

And this is only a day of pure sunlight.

Lord, I don't want to settle for groping along with a pin light

when You *are* the light.

I don't want a little obscure religion

when You *are* the truth.

I don't want to grovel in dim passageways of an underground life
    when I could be feeling the open rays upon my soul
        beside the sea of Your grace.
I know that means exposure.
    I'll risk that, Lord.
        Expose what You will in me.
            It will only strip away more self-protective layers
                so that I can bask, clean and forgiven,
                    in the warmth of Your love.
Love—light; light—love.
    It's all the same.
        It's what You are.
I will not fear Your nature.
    Perfect love dispels fear.
        Perfect light illumines everything,
            including me.
                Shine. Love. Warm.
                    Amen.

43
So often I pray for direction

Jesus, so often I pray for direction,
 for wisdom,
  for revelation
   as to the path I should take.
Thank You for showing me
 that You are perfectly willing to give me
  momentary direction, wisdom or illumination.
But, oh, how much more of all these things I could have
 if I would just seek You—Yourself!

You aren't some wisdom; You *are* wisdom.
You don't just give an indication of direction;
    You are the direction I should pursue.
You don't just illuminate the path;
    You are both the path and the light that shines on it.
You're so much more sufficient than the various gifts I might seek;
    You are the gift.
I don't want to lose sight of this
    and just nibble away at Your qualities;
        I want to have You—to have You embrace me.
Then I will have more than enough wisdom,
    knowledge, peace, illumination and direction.
All these I have in abundance
    when I have You.

44

Someone I love
is dying

Lord, someone I love is dying.
I've learned that dying doesn't happen all of a sudden
    any more than being born does;
        it's a process.
There are signs and indications,
    sometimes false contractions and pains,
        but the exact time can't be predicted—
            even estimated, really.
And coming into and going out of this world
    is not an easy thing.
But these are adventures
    like no other in the life between.
No one can accurately chart the courses
    or predict the experience.
        Birth and death are unique to each person.
Thank You, Lord, for the privilege
    of walking through this passage.

As hard and sometimes agonizing as it is,
    I wouldn't want to miss it.
To touch eternity so intimately—
    to hand off a hand I'm holding into the very hand of God
        changes me.
The glitter of glory lands on my face, too,
    and changes the way I see things.
I remember watching my grandbabies being born,
    emerging from the embryonic fluids
        all powdered with the rich, white coating of birth.
I wanted to turn my face
    from the agony my daughter was experiencing,
        but the fascination of that moment
            and her need for someone who'd "been there"
                kept me so engaged,
                    a thousand horses
                        could not have pulled
                        me away.
        My love for these two—my child and her child—
        held me.
Now the labor of death tells me
    that soon the passage door is opening
        to a place where an aging body
            will not be needed anymore.

I feel that what seems to be "going away" from here
    must in reality be a birth into a new place.
Someone—and maybe several someones—
    will be waiting, reading the signs,
        and anticipating.
For them and for me
    the door will be open just long enough
        for me to glimpse the eternal
            and for them to have a strange moment
                of remembering another time, another place.
As heaven sent us one of its treasures
    when those sweet babies were born,
        we are now sending a treasure
            we have held dear,
                trusting our loved one to other arms,
                    other hearts.
Thank You, Lord.
    Only at a birth or at a death do we get real about life.
    Help me remember.

45
Today I don't know what to say to You

Lord, today I don't know what to say to You.
I've tried listening, instead,
    but I can't hear what You're saying.
Our friend's bright young son—
    just becoming a jet pilot
        after finishing aviation college
        and so full of promise—
            fell from a mountain in the Alps
                where he and a buddy were
                mountain climbing.

I don't know what to say to these parents,
  I don't know what to say to our children,
    and I don't know what to say to You.
Show me how to sort out my faith in all this.
I know You don't owe us an explanation,
  but we still can't help asking
    for enough understanding
      to go on praying.
I am not asking for these sorts of human tragedies to make sense.
      The laws that govern gravity
        and cause and effect are already in place.
I'm only asking to see You more clearly in the center of the pain,
      bringing peace.
You are teaching us how fragile human life is
  and how *eternal* eternal life.
Help me to embrace life for this family
  while we struggle with the realities of death
    when today, I don't quite know how.

46
Again I say "thank You" for morning

Again I say "thank You" for morning.
Each morning is a baby born,
    a seedling sprouting,
        a clean sheet of paper.
Each morning is a fresh start and a mystery to explore.
Today, Lord, I explored a small dirt lane
    that led through a stand of virgin pines
        where no logger's saw,
           in the pursuit of progress,
              has ever toppled
                these proud conifers.

Their straight, black trunks were contrasted
    against the unspoiled white bark of paper birches.
The lake they surround was still and veiled in morning mist.
There, far from the madding crowd
    was just the private performance of loons
        calling to the wood ducks and Canadian geese.
Wherever geese and whistler swan exchange morning secrets,
    I am at home.
Do these timid and magnificent creatures
    nestle in the reeds on eternal shores?
This new page of morning,
    I will fill with praise and thanksgiving.
Thank You, Lord, that I can hold this pen—
    this is Your sweet gift to me.
May the love letter I write on the page of this day
    make Your great heart glad.

47
Panic rises
in my throat

Lord, panic rises in my throat
    whenever I stop to let myself realize
        that I may have to live in a silent world.
How I love to hear the music—
    not just of instruments and singers,
        but of life itself.
I am memorizing today the cadences
    of my grandchildren's musical inflections:
        Madeleine's little crescendos of delight,
          Lee's exciting movement of ecstasy
             over a piece of copper encrusted quartz
                he's finding on a copper country shoreline.
I replay in my mind Will's authoritative oration
    about all the cars ever used in *007* movies—
        their make, year, model and customizing packages.

I savor Jesse's sweet singing of all his "America songs"
  at the top of his little patriotic voice,
    but sitting with his back to me and his mother
      because he is so shy, fragile and impassioned—
        like a great movement of the symphony.
I can't help wondering how their grown-up voices
  will sound and if I'll ever hear them.
And I worry, Lord,
  about a life as a lyricist
    who can no longer write words to hug the music
      like two lovers on the dance floor.
And will I be able to hear with my heart
  the words my lover can no longer whisper in my ear
    as he holds me?
Lord, my life has been so rich with sound.
Help me to be so grateful
  that should I never hear another tone,
    my life, my head and my heart
      will still be filled with music.

48
Our country is in danger

Lord, our country is in danger
    and all of us are wondering
        what there is for us to do.
We feel weak and vulnerable.
    We are no longer in control.
        Yet we are singing again—
            the patriotic songs,
                the hymns,
                    the songs of truth.
    We are praying again—openly . . .
        on street corners,
            in city squares,
                in football fields,
                    in churches.
And we are being kind again to each other,
    to strangers,

to other drivers in traffic,

to those ahead of us in line at the grocery.

Could it be that our national arrogance

and pride in our power and control

have kept us from You

and from each other?

When we are in control and full of pride as individuals,

You cannot speak to us;

we cannot hear.

When we are arrogant and self-sufficient,

You can't lead us or give us divine wisdom

for the life issues that so easily destroy us

and our families.

Today, Lord, through the pain and devastation,

I praise You.

I praise You for using even this chaotic time

to let us remember there is goodness

in our hearts and a longing to know You.

Hold us like a mother holds her babies.

Teach us.

And lead us back to Yourself

And to each other.

Then You can heal our land.

49
It is harvest time

Lord, it is harvest time.
The ripe fields are being cut,
    their full grains carried by conveyors
        into waiting trucks,
            then driven off to storage bins.
Huge wagons loaded with baled grasses
    move like awkward prehistoric animals
        through the country roads, groaning
            with the weight of their burden.
Apples and pears,
    sweet and full,
        are sorted into wooden crates
            to be the central joy of craft festivals.
Root vegetables are being dug
    and hidden in dark cellars against the threat of winter.

Everywhere the reaping of fruit
    and grains
        and grasses
            celebrate the faithful work of spring planting
                and hot summer cultivation.
This, Lord, is the season to rejoice,
    the season to enjoy,
        the season to rest from labor and to dance
            in streets and country roads—
                around warm bonfires.
I feel it in my bones, Lord.
I, too, am entering the season of harvest.
For so long I have wondered what I would be when I grew up.
For so long I have done, as faithfully as I knew,
    just what the day demanded of me:
        daily tasks, tending children, meeting deadlines,
            passing out love, finishing routines.
All of the while I felt as if one day I would "turn out"—
    do something special—
        be something when I grew up.
Now, half a century of my days have passed
    doing "regular" things the best I knew.

I smell the smoke of autumn fires,
    and feel the days shortening.
I hear the rustle of "gathering in."
I can see now, that the daily *being* was what I was to do.

Even now, my days are so "regular,"
    my chores so unspectacular.
Yet I feel a festival in the air.
My grandchildren dance in the leaves on the hillside.
My husband hurries home to be warmed
    by hot soup and a fire in the kitchen hearth
        and by our well-tested love.
My work has, on wings of its own,
    found its way into places I will never go,
        but joy has returned on the wind to sing at the festival.
Yes, this is harvest time.
The fruit is ripe and sweet.
Help me, Lord, to see the life You've given me
    in a new and joyful perspective.
Help me to embrace the process of seasons.
May the harvest bonfires be a sweet incense to Your nostrils, too.

50
This day of national Thanksgiving

This day of national Thanksgiving
 I have personal gratitude to bring to You,
  For treasures on a very personal level:
  For the fire in the kitchen hearth this man I love
   kept burning through the night;
  For the hodge-podge of wonderful objects—
   furniture, pictures and child-art wall hangings—
    that make up this home's cache of memories;
  For the tables set by our sweet daughters
   and the ghosts we see of those
    who have sat in these same chairs over the years,
     talking, laughing, crying, pouting, praying;
  For the bubbles I feel in my stomach
   just knowing that any moment
    children will burst through the door.

They will run to throw their arms around my legs,
children full of excitement for this happy day;
For the memory of those so dear
who were once so much a part of this day—
now thankful to be around *Your* big table;
For the pain You've brought us through,
that distilled into victory,
making this and every moment sweeter
like the sap of a tree, bled into a silver pail,
then boiled around the clock
to make the golden nectar we call maple syrup.
Each drop is a big price—yet so sweet.
For Your presence, Lord,
that is the fire to distill,
the breeze to cool,
the storm to bend us low,
the sunshine to draw us upward.
No wonder our forefathers took such risks
and even died for the promise of a soil
on which they could kneel in repentance
and a clear space into which they could
freely speak their gratitude
and worship to You.

51
It is Advent

It is Advent.

I am waiting—waiting for Your coming, Lord.

There are so many places where I wait for Your coming.

You came to Bethlehem,

    that tiny place of an almost forgotten promise.

You came to Nazareth, an in-no-way spectacular town,

    and You came to Bethany, Capernaum and Jerusalem.

There are places in my life that await Your coming.

Here—where Your message of reconciliation is so needed—

    or there—where Your tears

    could fall like they did over Jerusalem—

I need You to come where it would take at least a choir of angels

    to make the dullest of hearts aware of something eternal.

I wait for Your entrance into those dark places of disbelief—
    the crude and mundane corners of my existence
        so in need of starlight illuminations.
Come where there is little privacy, comfort or warmth—
    where animals feed and lowly service is offered.
How many times have I plunged headlong
    into the celebration of Your coming
        without being assured of Your actual arrival?
I have gone more days than three
    "assuming You to be in our presence."
But Advent is not for scurrying or for assuming.
    It is for waiting.
May I recognize You when You come
    not as the peak moment of our preplanned celebration,
        but as the subtle surprise,
            the simple object of wonder,
              the God of small things.
I wait. Come, Lord Jesus, come.

52
My body
is throbbing
from fatigue

Lord, my body is throbbing from fatigue
    from all the Christmas preparations.
When I stop to consider the Messiah and His coming,
    I can't stop my mind.
I keep making mental lists of details,
     names I want to remember,
        things I have yet to do
           and foods I must buy or prepare.
But I am not complaining, Lord.
I love having a reason to do special things in Your name
    for people I love.
I am grateful that Your coming makes the whole world sing!

The business of Christmas brakes us all—
even those who don't know You for themselves—
from the craze of commerce for profit and accomplishment
and turns our attention to others.
The bell-ringers of the Salvation Army
have become as much a part of the joy
as Santa at the mall.
And although the crèche can no longer be assembled in the city square,
more of us are taking time to tell the children
why we make the manger and its tiny Occupant
such a part of our homes.
I feel the urgency more than ever as a new century is emerging
to make for another generation
a celebration that will make this
the most important event of the year.
This must not become just another day
or even just another holiday.
We must tell each other and the children
that this Babe in a manger
was and is
the coming together of heaven and earth.
But, Lord, help me keep that focus in my own heart.

Help me remember that there is nothing of value
        that doesn't demand sacrifice and effort.
You Yourself came on a quiet night in a small town,
    but it wasn't the idyllic, effortless night
        depicted in the windows.
There was blood and water and pain.
There were insufficient provisions and fear.
There were visitors at a time when Mary must have wanted privacy.
From then on, You were putting Your own needs as a human being
    on the back burner for the Big Picture.

So, it is not out of character for
    Christmas to be wonderful and demanding,
        a time when fatigue and effort are invested
            for a few amazing moments of glory.
            It is for love.
All this day, let me remember—it is for love.

53
On this new day
of the New Year

Lord, on this new day of the New Year I am thankful—
    perhaps most that last year is over
        and a new page has been turned.
I know the moment that marks a new year
    is in reality no different from any other moment.
Each moment gives me a chance to make a better choice,
    take a bigger risk,
        avoid a careless word,
            and embrace a glorious joy.
But sometimes we need a sacrament—
    a party, an event, a mark on the national calendar—
        to shake us from our routine.
We need a landmark,
    a finish line,
        a line in the dust that says,
            "Here. Here is the place to begin."

So, I am thankful for this moment.
This New Year's Day is a closure to pain,
an opening to joy,
a celebration of past victories,
a funeral for past failures,
an open door to exciting and terrifying possibilities,
a back-turning on all
that would drag us downward.

This is a moment.
I choose to love it.
I will do the hard thing today.
I will speak the truth today.
I will forgive and offer grace today.
I will receive forgiveness and give it today.
I will not be cynical today.
I will laugh freely like a child
at what I see,
at myself,
at the sheer loveliness of life.

Today I ask for no burning bushes or eruptions of Sinai.
I do ask for the eyes
to see the bushes already aflame
with awesome frozen beauty
glistening like diamonds in the air.

I ask for ears to hear the voice of God
 in the thunder.
I ask for the sensitivity
 to feel the pulse of the universe
  when I press my breast against the warm sand
   on the beach.
May I taste the honey
 on the purple roadside clover
  and the sweet tender end
   of the stems of native grasses.
May I thrill to the gentle touch
 of snow landing on my cheek,
  laugh when my nostrils send smoke rings of steam
   into the morning air.
Today may be as hard as yesterday,
 but make me a new woman in the living of it.
Tomorrow may be as glorious as my best memory.
 Make me a new woman to celebrate it.
Thank You.
That's all I have to pray.
Thank You.

54
It's a new day

Lord, it's a new day.
It's a new year, too,
    and a new decade ,
       a new century,
          a new millennium.
There certainly has never been in my lifetime a better time
    to start something,
       become something,
          do something new!
Yet, as I step over the line into such a major moment in history,
    I bring the same old me.
    I bring my old habits.
    I bring my same old body
       with its same bumps and knobs and wrinkles.
    I bring my same history and circle of relationships.
    I bring my expectations of myself and others,
       both realistic and unrealistic.

Lord, *new* is easy to talk about, but it's hard to come by.

Only You can make me new.

And only You can help me keep and treasure what's old and precious.

Only You can show me what I should keep and treasure
>
> and what I should discard and change.

Lord, You are teaching me
>
> that Your work in my life is not a resolution
>>
>> but a process.

All things—good, bad—regular, exciting—
>
> joyful, painful—routine, innovative—

All things work together to make me good,
>
> to make me what You want me to be.

Lord, it is easy for me to ask You to make me new this new year.

It is harder for me to ask You to make me consistent,
>
> enduring,
>>
>> patient,
>>>
>>> and submissive
>>>>
>>>> to what You're up to in my life.

But I do ask it.
>
> Make me, Lord, the well-shaped vessel
>>
>> You're already molding with the tools of life—
>>>
>>> the very things I sometimes ignorantly pray
>>>>
>>>> that You will remove from my days.
>>>
>>> This new year, I ask for trust and faith
>>>>
>>>> in what You're already doing in me.

55
This second day of the New Year

This second day of the New Year, the journey continues.
The star promises that the Messiah
    is already a reality in this earthen world,
        and hints that there are those who have found Him—
            some have even embraced Him.
Yet for even those who are wise enough to seek,
    this day is a desert day of dust and sand,
        plodding and enduring—until the star stops.
Most of us believers—who travel in caravan—
    visualize as we go where that star-place will be.

We can't help feeling that the place must be wonderful—
    an oasis, a resort, a fine abode fit for a King.
Like those first travelers,
    we are way too literal minded
        to keep focused on the wonder
            of the Incarnate One, Himself—
                that He *is* the wonder.
Will we be disappointed with the destination of this day's journey
    when we find no place spectacular?
Will we, like the poet, miss the glory of the summit
    because of bramble distractions?
Lord, today as every day, the hope of finding You on my journey—
    that starring promise—
        guides and pulls me along the dusty way.
Satisfy my seeking heart with the pleasant reality of Your sweet Self,
    resting there in the familiar surroundings of common things.
And, Lord, fill me with gratitude
    for Your provisions along my way to You.

56
How I love the starkness of January

Lord, how I love the starkness of January.
Oh, I love the lushness of June, too,
    the trees lavishly clothed in green,
    the outrageously vibrant greens of grasses,
    the bursting color of wildflowers and birds,
    the blue, blue of the summer sky.
But in January, we see the strong bones that hold it all together;
    the skeletons of the giant maples and oaks—
        black against the pale, grey sky;
    the brave sticks of bushes and undergrowth
        that have groaned all summer from the weight of foliage
    the animals that called their branches "home";

and the square and rectangular shapes of houses lining the streets,
    raw shelter for families who stay warm inside the walls
        built against the winter chill.
Thank You for the framework of all things:
    the law that protects us and holds up our freedoms;
    the social systems, like hospitals, schools, government structures;
    and churches that hold together
        the communities of breathing flesh
            and give us shape and strength.
Thank You for the grace of Your hand,
    the mercy, hope, love,
    and yes, the law that holds together the whole universe
        and all beyond, the galaxies unending.
Without You, we are just leaves and thistledown
    which "today is and tomorrow is thrown into the furnace."
Forgive our arrogance.
Thank You for the revelation of January
    that it is only in You
        that we "live and move and have our being."

57
Thank You
for this rare
week of listening

Thank You, Lord, for this rare week of listening.
Thank You, too, that You don't require silence and solitude
    before You speak to me,
        because these are not the regular commodities of my life.
Often in my noisiest places I feel You turning my face toward You
    like a child does when she needs someone to pay attention.

You turn my face to You with a sunset,
  a song,
    a majestic storm,
      or a small child's giggle.
Sometimes in a crowded place
      you whisper in my ear
        direction, warning, advice or sweet endearments
          for no other reason
            than I need so to hear them.
But this week, Lord, You have given me a quiet space
    away from other voices.
      Here I have not felt guilty for choosing solitude;
      I have been comfortable with the silence.
There have been no Mount Sinai revelations;
    I only sense a turning in my spirit.
I keep remembering the haunting words:
    "He set His face toward Jerusalem . . ."
What I've sensed is less a call to action
    and more a setting my face toward . . .
      Thank You.

58
Thank You
for my family

Lord, thank You for my family—
    not just my husband and three beautiful children,
        but for my parents and dear sister who told me all my life
           that I had a purpose and was of value,
                not for what I accomplished,
                    but for the person I am.
In the years since we lived together—the four of us—
    so much has happened in my life
        to make me doubt my value and question my purpose.
Yet somewhere deep in the fiber of my being,
    I have been sustained and empowered
        by the knowing that God created me a thing of value,
           precious to Him and important for my own sake.

When I have failed and betrayed my own expectations and the
expectations of others,
  I was saved from despair by this firm awareness
    of God's gift of grace through His own Son to me
      because I am loved by the One who truly knows me
      and purely loves me.
Today, Lord, my sister is in pain.
  I would so willingly bear this for her if I could.
  At least today, Lord, may I be able to remind her
    how loved she is,
    how infinitely she matters
      to You and to me.
We are all there is left of our family,
  at least here on earth.
But somehow pain brings us even closer
to the eternal perspective of all things—
    and to each other.
Ease her pain, Lord,
  but even in the intensity of it,
    may she never doubt her worth
      or be tempted to throw in the towel because
        of the demands on her endurance.
May my love and Yours heal and strengthen her.
  Amen.

59
Where could I go from Your presence? (II)

"Where could I go from Your presence?"
So many times I've read the psalmist's words, Lord,
    to remind myself that You *are* present,
        even in the places and times that seem forsaken and alien.
But here in the mountains, in the woods,
    it's easy to remember and feel You near.
Thank You for moments in places where
    Your creation is still pure enough
    to bear Your thumbprint.
How my husband and I needed this small two-day respite
    from the demands of our regular life!

We needed to be able to drink coffee on the screened-in porch
    and not have to answer the phone.
We needed to have a whole conversation
    about something besides demands of scheduling,
        problems in our work, family needs . . .
            Just to laugh is such a healer.
We needed to hold each other
    and make love,
        to sleep until we woke up without being awakened
            by an appointment or an immediate concern.
And thank You for ears to hear
    the morning symphony of birds in the trees,
    noses to smell spring awakening the earth,
    eyes to watch the dogwoods bloom and the leaves unfold.
Yes, Lord, I know we cannot go anywhere
    where You are not there,
    but thank You for the days like today
        when Your presence is the *main* awareness,
            And the breeze seems to be Your very breath!

60
My daughter
is in labor

Lord, my daughter is in labor.
The pain brings the most result;
    it nudges this little one on
        into the narrow confines of the birth canal;
       when the pain halts, hesitates—
          gained progress is lost;
She is discouraged when the pain subsides
    and the rhythm of contract-release, contract-release
      eases off and the child retreats.
         Yet she dreads the pain, fears it.

She asks if there is another way,
    if she can get out of this.
How can I tell her that the pain is the good news of progress—
    that it brings a healthier baby?
This descent down the birth canal is exercising his lungs,
    making him strong,
        and bringing them both
            closer to triumph—and ecstasy.
I will not tell her just now that this reality is also a metaphor—
    It is a shadow, a picture of a lifelong process of "birthing"
        and the pain, the glory of guiding him
            into another brave new world.

61
Father of the rain

Father of the rain,
 make me clean and help me not to duck for shelter
  but to embrace the cleansing.
Help me to love Your rain in all its forms:
 the mist that comes almost imperceptibly
  bringing such gentle moisture to shriveled cells
   that even the most fragile are not damaged
    but irrigated and enlivened.
 the fog, even more gentle than the mist,
  enfolding the dry spirit
   in a thick comforter of refreshment.

the steady rain that sets in during the night
   and continues all day,
      soaking everything to the very taproots.
the deluge that continues to wash away accumulations of debris,
   that overflows the dams men have constructed
      that reroute the streams on their way to the sea.
And, Lord, help me to even embrace the storms
   that shake me from my attachments,
      that bend and test me;
         they make me realize I am at Your mercy.
It was Your mercy that placed me here in the first place,
   and it is by Your mercy that I survive.
      Rain on me, Lord. Come, sweet rain.

62
Your Word says that in You we live

Lord, Your Word says
  that in You we live and move and have our being.
Philosophers have talked about our Ground of Being,
  the Source of Being
    but what You said was broader, higher, deeper.
Today, I am longing for wisdom.
  I keep finding my prayers focusing on this deep need
    and my words asking for this singled-out quality.
But if I live and move and have my being in You,
  wisdom surrounds me, protects me, speaks for me.
    Give me an awareness of this.
      Quiet my spirit with this knowing.
      Give me peace in it.
      Direct my actions and words within Your wisdom.
In that wisdom, give me the courage to trust
  when I can't see the outcome.
I choose to trust Your surrounding Self.
  Please make it real for me.

63
There are glimpses
of Your Body united

There are glimpses, Lord, of Your Body united
    and these glimpses are beautiful.
They let me know that this harmony, health and peace are possible,
    and, in spite of other times that shatter this vision,
        You will draw us like a magnet to Yourself.
There will be a time
    when all the broken and dispersed pieces of Yourself
        will come together in beautiful reality.
Lord, sometimes I feel as if I'm living in the valley of dry bones—
    surrounded by parched and bleached body parts
        disconnected from each other,
            unable to perform the simplest function of the living.

But then I hear a voice and a sweet wind brushes my face
like angel wing tips in a dream.
I see a strange movement.
I feel an innate desire for being connected
moving through the bones:
a song sung in harmony,
an embrace between two who thought they had
nothing in common,
a move to forgive before forgiveness is requested,
a meltdown of the spirit in some small group
studying Your Word.
I feel it then in my own bones—
a pull drawing me to the Head of focus.
I sense a warming in the marrow, a kindling of fire.
These times make me dare to trust
that the dislocated body parts will not only adjoin,
they will form the body of a beautiful Bride,
breathless with infatuation,
as she walks with perfect grace toward her Groom.

64
The aspens are still

The aspens are still.

   The pines are silent.

      Only the river rushes from the thawing mountaintop snows

        to the thirsty valley of the dry summer.

The air is cool and unobstructed by humidity or pollution of man.

The breath of all creation is on the intake . . . and holding.

I, too, inhale, filling my lungs with the clear mountain air.

Sometimes, Lord, I forget to breathe almost.

My life is so full, I forget to take a deep breath

   as I race from one of my lives to another.

But here You remind me to inhale,

   breathe deeply

      and fill my lungs with clean air

        and my consciousness with beauty.

My ears, I fill with nature sounds—nothing mechanical.
My eyes inhale, too,
    pulling in all the mountains,
        pines,
            streams,
                and sky they can hold.
Lord, let my soul breathe deeply, too.
I would inhale Your presence, Your Being,
    into my being.
May I exhale only praise,
    music,
        encouragement,
            and joy.
I would like to be what You promised:
    To be "alive with Your life,"
        That "I might come to share in the very being of God."

65

The news is full of the huge power outage in New York

Lord, the news is full of the huge power outage in New York
    and clear into the Midwest—Detroit, Cleveland, Toronto.
The cities are in darkness.
Commuters are caught in underground subway tunnels
    and on bridges above the rivers
        or arrested in whatever activity in which they were engaged
            and stopped on their way to destinations.
The life they knew is artificially maintained—
    artificially heated and cooled
        and artificially lit,
            artificially reached by elevator or escalator.
The residents are far-removed from the source of food;
    the windows in tall apartment buildings don't open,
        the structure built to assume there will be no need
            for fresh, cool air or a fire to warm one's hands.

How short the supply of water, food, medical supplies and
    provisions would be if all the people
        who work in the city were trapped there.
Yet how confidently they carry on from day to day
    trusting a system that is destined
        someday, someway to fail.
I'm like them, too, Lord.
So many times I travel far
    and operate in naïve confidence that I am self-sufficient,
        yet *You* are the Source of light,
            warmth and sustenance.
You are family and shelter, food for my soul.
Without You, I would very soon exhaust my puny supplies
    and find myself stranded—hungry, weary, and alone.
Thanks for reminding me today
    that when I depend on my own resources,
        a power outage is inevitable.
Keep me safely connected to Your inexhaustible supply.

66
I've been alone for a week

Lord, I've been alone for a week.
In trying to find solitude to write and think,
    to read and listen to You,
I also found moments of loneliness and despair.
The despair comes from getting still enough
    to become aware of all the things I cannot change.
For most of the looming issues in my life, I see no solution.
Someone wrote a song that says,
    "tears are a language God understands."
Is that true?
Do You hear the words that won't come?
Do You answer prayers we can't even articulate?

I've counseled others, giving them all the Scriptures
    like the ones that say You intercede for us
        in "groanings that cannot be uttered."
I've told others that You not only know our hearts,
    but the hearts of those who break our hearts.
But when it comes to grasping and accepting
    those promises for myself, especially when the problems
        have been unresolved for so long,
            I fumble through the fog of faith.
Lord, give me something to hold on to,
    some small evidence that You are working for all our good
        in spite of my lack of sight.
I do trust You. I have no one else to go to.
My history with You is as long as I've been alive.
So, I ask You to calm my spirit.
I don't have to have answers, but I would like to ask You for peace.
The rest I'll have to say with tears and silence.
    I don't know anything to say.

67
The laughter
of children

Lord, the laughter of children
    blends with the groans of the aging in my days,
        as I celebrate summer and family
            both by making new memories
                and saying goodbye to old ones.
I am the generation between.
I plan picnics with grandchildren and grown children
    on the same days I take my afternoons or mornings
        to tend to those in the hospital.

I make lists of things to pick up at the store
    that include pool toys
        and nursing supplies.
Today I will be thankful for the perspective this gives
    into where I have come from and where I am going.
I will let these days teach me to treasure the moments I have . . .
    with the children,
        with the aged.
I will glean wisdom from both and bring joy to both if I can.
    And I will see the whole life process as a gift—
        every passage of it!
And today I will love the journey that is mine
    and stoop to pick up jewels along my path.

68
For the tastes
of summer
I give thanks

For the tastes of summer I give thanks:

- for swollen red tomatoes that explode their wonder
    into my mouth,

- for berries and peaches,
    pears and apples,
        and all the fruits of the harvest orchards
            and berry patches,
        I clap my hands with glee like a child.

- For color and textures in such wild variety
    that they make a circus of the summer table,
        and make every meal a glorious celebration,
            I thank You.

- For pies and cobblers, salads and compotes,
  for all the ordinary creativity this bounty inspires,
  I thank You.
- For recipes passed down that tie our tasting parties
  to all the generations who have gone before
  and join the hands in my kitchen to the hands
  in the kitchens of Michigan and Indiana,
  Missouri and Tennessee,
  Italy and Germany,
  Ireland and England,
  I thank You.

I dance my turn in the jig
  or reel or clog or hoedown
  around our well-worn table.

69
These last few days have been a joyous celebration

Lord, these last few days have been a joyous celebration of family.

    Four generations sat at the breakfast table

        talking and laughing,

            telling stories and breaking bread.

The two little men read the Scriptures they had chosen to share

        which included the Revelation promise

". . . and He shall wipe all tears from their eyes

        and there shall be no more sorrow or pain or dying . . .

            All things shall be made new."

Could it be that these moments around our wooden table

        in the trees at the cabin we built so long ago,

            might last forever?

Thank You for these sweet glimpses of life
    as You intended and will one day restore.
Thank You for the hope that at that Table there will be no one missing,
    no gnawing loneliness for someone separated from the rest.
And in that day we will all be free
    from our faults and failures
        and distilled into our purest selves.
We will all know that only these simple pleasures
    have survived the refining fire burn-off
        and our joy will be—
            as You promised—
                complete.
Today we may be short with each other.
We may get weary of forgiving and asking for forgiveness.
    We may be thoughtless or rude or selfish
        or oblivious of each others' needs and feelings.
But thank You for these last few simple, joyful days in the woods
    where You revealed a hint of how much we could love each other
        and how dear each one really is.
I will carry that diamond
    in the pocket of my heart today.

70
I thank You for this most amazing day

I thank You, Lord, for this most amazing day—
    for legs that move,
        for arms to reach,
            and hands that hold and touch.
Today the gift of breathing—
    a gift I seldom consider—
        has my attention.
Here in the wide protected natural lands of Wyoming
    where the air is crisp and clear,
        I fill my lungs to capacity with each breath,
            as I walk or ride horseback
                through Your amazing handiwork.
Lord, someone I love has a malignant tumor in his lung.
    I watch him struggle to breathe,
        hear his labored effort,
            see him clinging to his life-saving tank of oxygen.

Lord, this man has lived an active outdoor life,
  farming,
    gardening,
      helping his neighbors
        with the plowing of snow or of fields,
          mowing the hay,
            enjoying the blessed simple things of life.
I ask You for him this pristine morning
  a few more days, weeks or months of breathing.
    I ask it with every intake of this fresh mountain air—
And as I do,
  I breathe this air in gratitude for this
    and a thousand other automatic functions of this body
      You created so fearfully
        and wonderfully perfect.
Today, too, as I lift up my eyes unto the hills,
  I will remember
    that my help comes not from the hills,
      as beautiful as they are,
        but from the One who made them
          and all other wonders—
            noticed and unseen.

71
There is a stirring
in my soul

Father, there is a stirring in my soul
　　that began years ago about who You really are
　　　　and how that reality can be shown
　　　　　　to the people in our town,
　　　　　　　　in our world.
Even in America
　　most of our children's friends
　　　　have no experiences with belief in You that affects choices
　　　　　　and how life is lived on a daily basis.
My generation had parents who loved us,
　　or grandparents who could bring us home to faith
　　　　when they were buffeted by life.

For my children's generation there isn't even a grandparent.
  They, too, are divorced
      and fragmented
          with no stability.
This generation of kids
  creates their own pseudo-family relationships
      because they are so starved for the real thing.
This may be living with a boyfriend,
  hanging out with groups of other damaged kids,
      or following some strange spirituality
          in order to belong *somewhere.*
I go to church,
  and though I am so familiar
      and comfortable with the form
          because I've grown up with it,
I am not comfortable that all the houses we pass to get there—
  even if we go the back roads through the country—
      are full of people who are working in their yards,
          yelling at their kids,
              or sleeping in 'til noon.
Church shouldn't be a place we go.
It should be something we *are* to these people
  detached from our Sunday morning,
      and the ones across the street

or at our kids' workplace—
the university,
the office,
the parent-teacher conferences.
What should *being* church look like?
Maybe like a backyard cookout?
A coffee house on Tuesday midmorning
after the kids are delivered to school?
A girls' night out at the cabin in the woods?
A bonfire after soccer?
Isn't anywhere discussions are taking place about Jesus in our lives
and what the Bible says about where joy comes from *church*
because the Body is there?
Isn't it breaking bread together—
even if that bread is a hot dog bun—
if His Body is present?
I have a feeling church isn't something we "go to";
it should be the folks themselves
who go *from* our gathering
refreshed and inspired
to give themselves away
for something that lasts forever.
Are You troubling me, Lord?
Is there something You're crowding me into?

About the Author

Gloria Gaither is the author or coauthor of 42 books, numerous articles and published academic papers and literature. She has been inducted into the Gospel Music Hall of Fame and has been distinguished with honorary doctorates from six universities. She is the lyricist for over 700 songs written with her husband, composer Bill Gaither, several of which have received Grammy® and Dove® Awards. Together, they were named Songwriter of the Century in the field of Christian music. Gloria and Bill live in Alexandria, Indiana, where they began their lives together 45 years ago. She will tell you that their best contribution has been their three children and six grandchildren, who regularly crowd around the oak table in their big country kitchen to laugh and tell stories.

Index of Titles/
First Lines

Topical Index

🌿